Date: _______________

Created especially for you

Date: ____________________________________

Created especially for you

Everyone needs
'A Little Black Book'.
A place to write 'secret
things' and to write 'stuff'
that you think about and
want to remember - and
not want to remember.
'A Little Black Book' is that
prized and treasured
notebook
that you keep close to your
heart.
The 'Little Black Book' that
takes you on journeys of
memories - and prepares
you for the next one.
Everything you need will be
in here.

Created especially for
you.....

Date: _______________________

Date: _______________

Date: ______________________________

Created especially for you

Date: _______________________________

Date: ___________________

Date: _______________________________

Date: ___________________________________

Date: ______________________________

Date: _______________________

Created especially for you

Date: _______________________________

Date: _______________________

Date: _______________________________

Created especially for you

Date:

Date: ______________________________

Date: _______________________________

Date: _______________

Created especially for you

Date:

Created especially for you

Date: ___________________

Created especially for you

Date: _______________________

Date: _______________

Date: _______________

Date: _______________________

Created especially for you

Date: ______________________________

Date: ___________________________

Date: ___________________________

Created especially for you

Date: ______________________

Created especially for you

Date: ______________________________

Date: _______________________________

Created especially for you

Date: _______________________________

Created especially for you

Date: ______________________________

Created especially for you

Date: _______________________________

Date: ________________________________

Created especially for you

Date: _______________

Date: ______________________________

Date:

Created especially for you

Date: _______________________________

Date: ___________________________

Date: ___________________________________

Date: _______________________

Date:

Date: _______________________

Date: ______________________

Created especially for you

Date: ___________________________________

Created especially for you

Date: _______________________________

Created especially for you

Date: _______________________________

Date: ______________________________

Date: _______________________

Date: _______________________

Date: ___________

Date: _______________________________

Created especially for you

Date: _______________________________

Created especially for you

Date: _______________________________

Date: _______________________

Date: ___________________________

Created especially for you

Date: _______________________

Created especially for you

Date: _______________

Created especially for you

Date: ________________________________

Created especially for you

Date: _______________________________

Date: _______________________________

Created especially for you

Date: _______________________

Created especially for you

Date: _______________________________

Created especially for you

Date: _______________

Date: _______________________

Created especially for you

Date: ______________________________

Date: ______________________________

Created especially for you

Date: ______________________________

Date: _______________________

Date: ____

Date: _______________________________

Date: _______________________

Date: _______________________

Created especially for you

Date: _______________

Date: _______________________________

Created especially for you

Date: ___________________

Date: ______________________________

Created especially for you

Date: _______________________________

Created especially for you

Date: _______________________________

Created especially for you

Date: _______________________

Date: _______________________

Created especially for you

Date: _______________________

Date: _______________________

Date: _______________________

Date: _______________________

Created especially for you

Date: _______________

Date: _______________________________

Created especially for you

Date: _______________________________

Created especially for you

Date: _______________

Date: _______________________

Date: _______________________

Date: _______________

Date: ______________________________

Date: ____

Date: ______________________

Date: ______________________________

Date:

Date: _______________________________________

Date: ________________________

Date: ______________________________

Created especially for you

Date: ____

Created especially for you

Date: ______________________________

Created especially for you

Date: _______________________________

Date: _______________

Created especially for you

Date: _______________________

Date: _______________________

Date: _______________________________

Created especially for you

Date: ____

Created especially for you

Date: _______________________________

Created especially for you

Date: _______________________________

Created especially for you

Date: _______________________________

Created especially for you

Date: ___________________________

Date: _______________________________

Created especially for you

Date: _______________

Date: _______________________________

Created especially for you

Date: _______________________________

Created especially for you

Date: _______________________________

Created especially for you

Date: _______________________

Date: ___________________________________

Created especially for you

Date: _______________

Date: _______________________________

Created especially for you

Date: ______________________

Created especially for you

Date: _______________________

Date: ______________________________

Date: ______________________

Created especially for you

Date: _______________

Date: _______________________________

Created especially for you

Date: ______________________________

Created especially for you

Date:

Created especially for you

Date:

Created especially for you

Date: _______________________________

Created especially for you

Date: _______________

Date: _______________

Date:

Date:

Date: ________________________________

Created especially for you

Date:

Date:

Date: _______________________________

Created especially for you

Date: _______________________________

Created especially for you

Date: ____

Created especially for you

Date: _______________________________

Created especially for you

Date: _______________________

Created especially for you

Date: _______________________________

Created especially for you

Date: _______________________________

Created especially for you

Date: ______________________________________

Date: _______________

Date: _______________________

Created especially for you

Date: _______________________________

Date: _______________________

Created especially for you

Date: _______________________

Date:

Date: _______________________

Date: _______________________

Created especially for you

Date:

Date: _______________________

Created especially for you

Date: _______________________

Date:

Date: _______________________________

Created especially for you

Date: _______________________

Date: _______________________________

Created especially for you

Date: ___________________________

Created especially for you

Date:

Date: ___________________________

Created especially for you

Date: _______________________

Date: _______________________

Created especially for you

Date: ____________________

Date: _______________________________

Created especially for you

Date:

Date: _______________________________

Created especially for you

Date: ____

Created especially for you

Date: _______________________

Created especially for you

Date: _______________________

Created especially for you

Date: _______________________

Created especially for you

Date: _______________________

Date: _______________________________

Date: ____

Created especially for you

Date: _______________________________________

Created especially for you

Date: ______________________________

Created especially for you

Date: ______________________________

Date: ______________________________

Created especially for you

Date: _______________________________

Date: ______________________________

Date: _______________________________

Date: _______________________________

Created especially for you

Date: _______________________

Created especially for you

www.ingramcontent.com/pod-product-compliance
Lightning Source LLC
Chambersburg PA
CBHW052002150726
47999CB00004B/1485